Randolph Caldecott
The Children's Illustrator

by Marguerite Lewis

Published by Alleyside Press, A Division of Freline, Inc.
P. O. Box 889, Hagerstown, Maryland 21741

ISBN 0–913853–22–4

Printed in the United States of America

From *The Farmer's Boy*

Chapter 1

"Randolph, where are you?" Alfred called. He knew Randolph was there in the woods. It was his favorite spot. But, he would not answer.

Father had sent Alfred to fetch Randolph. "He is to come home at once," Father had ordered sternly.

"Randolph," Alfred called again. "Answer me. I know you are here."

Randolph had heard his younger brother calling. Flint flashed in his usually gentle blue eyes. His slender body stiffened, and he ran his fingers through his curly brown hair. He would answer when he was ready. First, he must complete the final strokes before the rabbit family heard Alfred thrashing through the woods and fled. A few lines and he was finished.

"I'm here," he called quietly. The mother rabbit jerked her ears. She looked up at Randolph, snatched the remaining carrot treat, and vanished into the brush. Her babies followed in a flash of bobbed tails.

"Oh, Randolph, why won't you ever answer me?" Alfred complained, approaching from behind. He peered at the sketch. "Randolph, that's good. How can you do so much with just a few lines? Those rabbits look real."

Alfred threw himself down beside Randolph. "Father says to come home at once. You were supposed to be home hours ago."

"All right," Randolph said, reluctantly closing his sketch pad and pocketing his pen. The boys left the woods and followed the lane back to the city.

They arrived at the old walled city of Chester, England, built on top of old Roman ruins before 1330. They entered at Eastgate Street and turned left onto

Bridge Street. Houses with continuous covered porches built at the first story lined both sides of the street. These houses were called the Rows.

Father's shop, where Randolph had been born ten years before on March 22, 1846, was halfway down the Rows. Father was a tailor and hatter, and the family lived in rooms above the shop.

"Well, it's about time." Father's voice was gruff. "I am getting tired of having to send Alfred to fetch you. There is work to be done. You must do your share, boy."

The shop was hot and smelled of moist wool. The windows were small, and little natural light filtered through. Randolph put away his sketch pad and went over to the pressing table.

John Caldecott shook his head and sighed. Randolph knew that sigh. He knew what his father was thinking. Raising boys was no easy task. His wife had died when Randolph was six and Alfred only four. Perhaps he should remarry. The boys needed a woman to look after them. Since a bout with rheumatic fever, Randolph had thought about nothing but reading and drawing. True, he was not strong. He could not run and play like the other children, and he tired very easily. Mr. Harris, the headmaster at King's School, had high praise for Randolph's academic ability. But, drawing was for idle people— people with money and nothing to do. It was not real work for a man. Father sighed again. Randolph looked up from his work. How he wished Father would understand.

The air was humid and sticky in the tiny bedroom that Randolph shared with Alfred. The open window gave no relief, and the odor of steamed wool permeated even the pillow. Randolph's thoughts turned to the countryside. "I wish I could live out in the country," he whispered to Alfred. "The air is so clean and cool there." Alfred didn't answer; he was already asleep. Randolph hated the dark, dank shop. The air clogged his throat, and breathing was so difficult. He thought about the next day. Mr. Harris had promised that Randolph could begin painting with watercolors when his lessons were finished. The lessons were easy, and Randolph enjoyed school. (He knew he was lucky; his Father let him stay in school. Most boys his age were already working at a trade.) The thought of watercolors was exciting. Usually, he sketched with pen and ink or a charcoal stick. Randolph loved to draw. He could not remember a time that he had not itched to draw. He had even tried to draw Mother from memory. The sketch was awkward, but it was the only likeness he had of her.

The next day at King's School, Mr. Harris placed before Randolph a set of watercolor paints.

"What will you draw?" he smiled. He was fond of this quiet, serious lad.

Randolph's blue eyes sparkled. "Animals," he answered. His fingers itched to begin but he controlled them for a moment, letting the memories stored in his mind appear before him. The bell for choir practice startled Randolph. The hour had seemed like only a few minutes. He left the paintings to dry and filed into the church with the rest of the boys.

The older students sat in the back of the canopied choir stalls. Randolph was fascinated by the intricate fourteenth century carvings on the stalls. Fortunately, he learned the hymns and responses easily and could study the lines and scrolls while responding automatically to the music. During lengthy sermons on Sundays, however, he heard not a word. He daydreamed over the exquisite work of those early artists, storing in his mind the lines and figures. He especially loved the carved scenes on the Dean's and the Vice Dean's stalls, showing the pilgrims praying for the powers of healing at the Shrine of St. Werburgh.

For days, Randolph practiced drawing animals, children, and scenes of his beloved countryside. Now, he was ready to try something different. The refectory, where school was held, was his favorite room in the cathedral. The walls were crisscrossed with carved beams. On a raised dais stood a magnificent carved pulpit, from which the early monks had read to the brothers during meals. Randolph thought of the silence, broken only by the droning words of the monk who was reading. He pictured the brown cowled monks spooning gruel into their mouths, eating only to stay healthy, not for enjoyment.

That afternoon, he drew the early refectory. A scene of shades of brown emerged—the almost black-brown of the carved beams, the medium brown of the rough plank tables, and the lighter brown of the monks' garb. The picture was drab. It was not right. Randolph mixed some colors and added some strokes and dabs. The scene came to life. Among the downcast shaved heads of the monks, one monk looked up, a mischievous quirk in his brown eyes. A squirrel lodged in the rafters. The carvings seemed to breathe, and the monk at the pulpit searched toward the heavens, with the light of inner joy in his smile.

Mr. Harris studied the drawing. He raised his head and looked hard at Randolph. His eyes returned to the drawing. He said nothing. Randolph squirmed. Did Mr. Harris not approve? Had it been wrong to interject a bit of gaiety, when the lives of the monks had been ones of total religious sacrifice?

The next day when Randolph entered the refectory, he discovered that the drawing had been framed and was hanging on the back wall.

"I wish to speak with you," said Mr. Harris in a low voice. "Please remain after the other boys leave."

At the end of the day, after the other boys had filed out, Mr. Harris beckoned Randolph to the painting.

"This is very good," he beamed. "I can see in my mind the life of the early monks. It is almost as if you had been there." He paused. "Randolph, you should go to art school. To the Chester School of Art."

"I doubt Father would approve, Sir," Randolph answered quietly. But, the sheer thought of going to art school brought a sense of wonder to his eyes.

"What about you? I'm asking you. Do you want to?" Mr. Harris asked.

"Oh yes, Sir." Randolph's eyes met Mr. Harris' eyes squarely.

"I shall come and talk with your father tonight." Mr. Harris stared again at the painting.

From *The Great Panjandrum Himself*

Chapter 2

Alfred had waited impatiently outside for Randolph.

"What did Mr. Harris want? Why did he ask you to stay behind? Did you get into trouble?" The questions tumbled out, all before Randolph could answer the first one.

"Do you think Father would let me go to art school? To the Chester School of Art?" Randolph answered with questions of his own.

Alfred cocked his head. "Art school? That costs money. How would it be paid?"

"I don't know," Randolph said. "Mr. Harris thinks I should go. He is coming to talk with Father tonight."

The boys walked along St. Werburgh Street. When they reached Eastgate Street, Randolph looked longingly to the right, where Eastgate Street led out of the city to the countryside. He turned, however, to the left and crossed Eastgate Street to Bridge Street.

"Are you going to tell Father that Mr. Harris is coming?" asked Alfred.

"What do you think?" Randolph ran his fingers through his hair. "Would it be best to tell him or just let Mr. Harris arrive?"

"Tell him." Alfred nodded his head. "Father doesn't like surprises."

Father was busy with a customer when they arrived at the shop. "Go up and start your homework," he told them. "I will be up shortly."

The boys said little during supper. When the meal was over and John Caldecott had lit his pipe, he asked, "Well, what is it? You boys are too quiet. What have you done now?"

"Father, Mr. Harris is coming to see you this evening," Randolph blurted out.

"I knew it. What have you done? Which one of you?" Father said, looking at Alfred.

"Mr. Harris thinks I should go to art school." Randolph drew back and watched his father.

"Art school, eh? Now the headmaster is encouraging you to waste time." John Caldecott shook his head. "Well, let him come. He may speak his piece. Not that it will do any good."

Mr. Harris arrived soon after and was closeted with Father for an hour. Randolph, waiting upstairs with Alfred, heard the front door close.

"Randolph," came Father's voice, "come here."

Randolph slowly descended the stairs.

Father shook his head, "I don't know what's come over me. Mr. Harris has a way with the words. You may go to the art school, every Saturday morning."

"How will we pay for it?" Randolph asked.

"You will pay for it by working in the shop, after school now and all day when school lets out for the summer." Father looked at Randolph. "Agreed?"

Randolph smiled. "Agreed, Father."

"Who knows," Father paused to light his pipe, "you may find you could like working in the shop. It's not a bad living."

Father and Randolph each kept their word. For a month, Randolph worked after school in the hot, sweaty shop. Then, he worked all day, except on Saturday and Sunday. He attended art school every Saturday.

"It's been worth it," thought Randolph, a year later. Relaxing in his favorite spot in the woods, he thought back over the year. He had learned a good deal about line and color and capturing the human figure on paper. Best of all, he had had someone to encourage him.

The teacher had taught him all he could, and now Randolph was on his own. "Practice, practice, and more practice is what you need now," the teacher told him. "I cannot teach you any more. I have not had enough training myself."

Randolph did practice. He drew pages of heads, faces, hands, and feet and pages of animals and woodland scenes. He loved to watch the young children at play and to try to capture their laughter and dancing on paper. His drawings were spare and sparse. One stroke conveyed a great deal, and every line counted. There were no excess lines or strokes.

After a year at the art school, Randolph continued to attend King's School, where he was appointed head boy (the student assistant to the headmaster), and to work at the shop.

"You look tired, Randolph," Father remarked late one Saturday. "You better take tomorrow off, and go out of the city."

Randolph escaped to the clean, cool air of the woods. He knew that Father was concerned about his future. What would he do? There was no way he could work in the shop for the rest of his life. What would Father decide to have him do when he was finished at school? Randolph would have no choice in the matter. It was a father's responsibility to secure a position for his son.

Mr. Harris was also concerned about Randolph's future. "You'll be leaving here soon," he said to Randolph, late in the spring. "Will you continue your studies?"

"I'm to go to work," Randolph said. "Father got me a position as clerk at the Whitchurch and Ellesmere Bank in Whitchurch."

"Oh, and how do you feel about that?" asked Mr. Harris.

"I think I shall like it. It's better than working in the shop," answered Randolph. "Father's family came from Whitchurch. He says the air is healthier there."

"What about your drawing?" Mr. Harris was concerned.

"I shall always draw," smiled Randolph. "I plan to live outside of town. There should be lots of new things for me to sketch."

A week after finishing at King's School, Randolph packed his belongings, made his farewells, and left for Whitchurch.

From *The House that Jack Built*

Chapter 3

The twenty-mile trip south to Whitchurch was exciting. Randolph had never been more than a couple of miles outside of Chester. The air was fresh and clean, and the small villages along the way delighted him.

Randolph found lodgings in the farmhouse of William and Charlotte Brown in Wirswall, a hamlet about two miles outside of Whitchurch.

"This will be fine," Randolph told Mrs. Brown. "Could I hire a horse sometimes? Riding is one of the few physical activities I can do. I will walk to the bank, but I would like to ride around the country."

Randolph liked his job as bank clerk. He enjoyed the work—adding sums came easily to him—and he enjoyed talking with the customers. But, one morning, Jim Etches, another clerk, approached Randolph's desk. "The manager wants to see you," he said.

When Randolph was seated, the manager looked up as he straightened a pile of papers in his hands.

"You have done your work well, Randolph. We are pleased with your progress," he said, shuffling the papers. "However, there is one small matter. Is this your work?" He showed Randolph the papers. Each was covered with sketches. There were squirrels and rabbits chasing each other around the edges of deposit slips. Country scenes decorated withdrawal slips, and profiles of clerks and customers peered at each other on the backs of envelopes. There was even a sketch of the manager on bank stationery.

"Not a bad likeness," the manager said, clearing his throat. "I shall give it to my wife."

Randolph reddened. He ran his fingers through his hair. "Those are mine, Sir," he admitted.

The manager handed the rest of the papers to Randolph. "In the future, I expect you to confine your artistic endeavors to your own time, outside of bank hours. And, change your desk blotter. It is not proper to have mice and hedgehogs dancing around a desk blotter in a bank."

Living in the country delighted Randolph. He always carried a pad of paper, and, while walking to and from the bank, he often paused to sketch a scene or an animal. His friends knew his passion for drawing and understood why he often arrived at work just in the nick of time or even a little late.

"Just in time," Jim would remark, as Randolph came rushing into the bank a minute before opening hours. "What caught your eye this time?"

"I kept your supper hot in the oven," Mrs. Brown would say. She was fond of Randolph. "It's been such a nice day. I thought you might be late."

It was the custom of the bank to carry on business at small village halls and at the homes of customers. Randolph was pleased when it was his turn to travel. He had grown into a tall, slender man. His blue eyes were still serious and his manner quiet. But, sparkle and a good sense of humor would flash in his eyes unexpectedly. The villagers welcomed him, whether he came on business or simply stopped for a chat while in the neighborhood.

On occasion, Randolph returned to Chester to visit his family. On one such visit in November of 1861, a great light filled the sky.

"Randolph," cried Alfred, returning home from a visit with friends, "the Queen Hotel is on fire." The Queen Hotel was a block square structure on City Road, just opposite the railway station.

Randolph grabbed his sketch pad and pens and joined Alfred in the Rows. They hurried up Bridge Street and turned left onto Watergate Street. As they neared City Road, they could see flames shooting into the sky.

Alfred ran ahead. Randolph watched for a minute, catching his breath. The running had nearly exhausted him. He knew the efforts to fight the blaze would be useless. The building was completely engulfed in flames. He took out his sketch pad and began to draw.

When Randolph returned to Whitchurch, he sent the drawing, along with an account of the event, to the *Illustrated London News*. The paper published the drawing on December 7, 1861.

Randolph's hands trembled as he saw his first work to appear in print. Everyone at the bank congratulated him, and customers came by, just to catch a glimpse of him.

Just about everyone in Chester knew about the article and picture. Randolph felt like a celebrity when he returned home for the Christmas holidays. Even Father was impressed.

Alfred was excited about the drawing, but he had a question: "The paper printed your name, but why did you not sign the picture, Randolph?"

"I did not expect it would be printed," replied Randolph.

"Will you sign your work from now on?" Alfred asked.

"Yes, but I will use only my initials," replied Randolph.

It was during that Christmas visit that Randolph learned of Alfred's plans to enter the Church when he finished at King's School.

"I have no one to leave the shop to," said John Caldecott, visually disappointed. "I should have remarried. Then I might have had more sons."

"You might have had daughters," laughed Randolph.

"True," mused John. "But, they might have had husbands. I will continue as long as I can, then I will sell the shop."

After the holiday, Randolph settled down again in Whitchurch. He continued to draw and enjoy good times with a small group of friends; however, there was no art or writers' group in Whitchurch. There was no one with whom he could discuss his work. He began to feel as if he was living in a vacuum. His days were spent at the bank; evenings and weekends were spent sketching or with friends.

Finally, in 1867, at the age of twenty-one, Randolph decided that he had to make a change. He had to be able to meet with other artists and to find another art school. He had worked too long on his own.

Earlier, on December 24, 1866, Randolph had met William Langford, Director of the Manchester and Salford Bank. Through Langford, Randolph applied for a job as a clerk at this bank and was hired.

When Randolph made his farewells to the people at the Whitchurch and Ellesmere Bank, he did so with reluctance. He had been happy there. He was exchanging a life of security in the country for one of confinement—being hemmed in again—in a city.

Mrs. Brown was sorry to have him leave; he had been a fine boarder. "Mr. Caldecott," she asked, "please, could you leave a sketch or two for me to hang on the wall? We have enjoyed having you with us. It would remind us of you."

"It would be my pleasure." Randolph was pleased.

On the day of his departure. Randolph presented Mrs. Brown with a trio of sketches, one each showing the farm, the family, and the surrounding countryside.

From *A Frog He Would A-Wooing Go*

Chapter 4

A new world unfolded itself to Randolph in Manchester. He enrolled in the evening division of the Manchester School of Art.

"A group of us are getting together tonight," a fellow student welcomed him. "Would you like to join us?"

Randolph began to participate in many evenings of discussions. The talks stimulated him. Seeing the talent of the other students encouraged him to copy his sketches in watercolors. He also began to practice clay modeling.

The habit of taking long walks in the country changed to taking long walks in the city. He wandered the dim and dusty streets sketching characters, buildings, and waterfront scenes.

Randolph joined the Brasenose Club, an organization dedicated to artistic endeavors. With friends, he enjoyed long horseback rides in the country. Around the city his favorite means of transportation, besides walking, was riding a horse and gig.

The polluted air of the city began to make his health worse. Manchester was a coal-burning, textile city. A dusty pall always hung low over the city, so he escaped to the country whenever possible.

"You should have your work exhibited," James Blower, another bank clerk, remarked one day, watching Randolph dash off a sketch during their lunch break.

"Some of the fellows at the Brasenose Club are having an exhibition next month," Randolph mused. "They have asked me if I wanted to be included. Maybe I will."

The following month, along with several other artists, Randolph exhibited his work, which contained paintings and sketches of both city and country life.

Encouraged by the favorable reviews of his work at that exhibition, Randolph sent some sketches to two weekly newspapers, the *Will O' the Wisp* and the *Spinx.* Both bought the sketches. Again, Randolph saw his work in print. From this time on, his work began to appear regularly in both newspapers.

Slowly, Randolph's job in the bank began to take second place in his life. He continued to do his work well, but his interest declined. Sketches appeared on deposit slips, withdrawal slips, and the backs of envelopes. He sketched customers and bank clerks instead of adding or subtracting sums. Rabbits and squirrels ran around his desk blotter.

Early in 1870, Randolph bundled his courage and his sketches together and visited London. He met with Thomas Armstrong, Art Director of the South Kensinger Museum and an established and respected artist. Armstrong was impressed with Randolph's work.

"If you leave your sketches with me, I would like to show them to Henry," he told Randolph. Henry Blackburn was the editor of *The London Society,* a popular magazine.

Although Randolph returned to Manchester, his visit made him realize how much he wanted to live in London. The opportunities to study, to learn, and to work in the company of well-known artists would be far greater in London than in Manchester.

Later in 1870, Blackburn bought several of the sketches Randolph had left with Armstrong and printed them in *The London Society.*

For two more years, Randolph worked at the bank. He saved his money and worked on a portfolio of sketches. In 1872, Randolph made his decision. He could no longer continue at the bank; he needed to go to London. Somehow, he would be able to make enough money painting and sketching. His needs were few. He was prepared to go hungry to be able to paint and draw full time.

Again, Randolph packed his belongings. Filled with worry mixed with a sense of excitement, Randolph set off for London.

From *The Milkmaid*

Chapter 5

Randolph need not have worried. He was accepted quickly into the art world of London. The city in 1872 was home to many well-known artists, writers, and editors. They welcomed the tall, quiet, and serious young man. Randolph was eager to learn and a willing student for the older, wiser, and more-experienced artists.

Lodgings were found for Randolph at 46 Great Russell Street. And, through Henry Blackburn, he met Sir Edward J. Poynter, a painter and member of the Royal Academy. Randolph enrolled in Poynter's class at the academy.

Henry Blackburn introduced Randolph to many other artists, and soon, Randolph found himself part of the group of artists that flourished in the city.

During his first year in London, Randolph was hired to paint decorative panels for Bank House, the home of wealthy Henry Ranshaw. Through this commission, he met Jules Dalou, a well-known French sculptor whose work Randolph greatly admired. Dalou made a deal with Randolph: "If you will help me learn the English language, I will help you with clay modeling."

Henry Blackburn, aware of Randolph's ability to sketch quickly, suggested that Randolph try illustrating news stories for the newspapers. For months, Randolph worked as a journalistic illustrator. He enjoyed the work, but it was not good for his health.

"You are looking tired, Randolph," Blackburn remarked, noticing his pallor and drawn features.

"I find meeting a deadline difficult," Randolph admitted. "I must be on the go constantly, whenever a story breaks, regardless of the hour. Then the drawing must be done from the sketch immediately. I don't know how much longer I can continue to work for the newspapers."

Blackburn, realizing the stress was too much for Randolph, had another suggestion. "Would you be interested in illustrating books on travel?" he asked. "That would relieve the time element."

Through Blackburn, Randolph received a commission to illustrate several books about the Harz Mountains in Europe. In the company of Blackburn and his wife, Randolph traveled through the mountains for a year, producing a diary of sketches. He returned rested and looking healthier.

The Harz Mountain sketches were the first of Randolph's work to appear in the United States. Selections from the books appeared in *Harper's New Monthly Journal* in June of 1873 and in the *New York Graphic* on September 16, 1873.

One day, shortly after Randolph returned to London, a man named James Cooper came to call on him. Cooper brought with him a copy of Washington Irving's *Old Christmas*. He had been trying for some time to find the right illustrator for the book. Cooper was an engraver. He hired Randolph to do the illustrations. When the book was published in 1875, it was evident that the memories Randolph had stored in his mind throughout his lifetime of sketching had been brought forth. The book was a great success, and Randolph illustrated several other books by Washington Irving for Cooper.

The work exhausted Randolph. He labored long and hard over each drawing. He practiced the art of leaving out. He often joked, "The fewer the lines, the less error committed." Every stroke counted. There were no excess lines or flourishes. He continued to sign his work with only his initials. The initials had to fit into the drawing or he would leave them out.

Randolph stated in a letter to his friend John Cooper, "I would rather leave out my initials, and I often do, than to have them interfere with the drawings. In these slight drawings, every line counts."

The initials appear to be three dimensional, with the *R* chasing the *C*. The initials blend in so well with the drawing that the viewer must look carefully to find them.

In 1876, he left London to spend a year in northern Italy and on the Riviera. His health was not good. When asked about his health, he always answered, "Quite well, thank you," but he was unable to climb two flights of stairs without stopping to rest. He had accepted a lifetime of poor health and seldom referred to or focused on it, except when he included himself in a drawing that called for a character of less than robust health. His sense of humor often caused him to poke fun at his own lack of physical strength.

After the year in Italy, Randolph thought that he had recovered enough to return to England. On his return, he began the work for which he is best remembered.

From *An Elegy on the Death of a Mad Dog*

Chapter 6

Randolph returned to England during an exciting time there. Many changes were taking place in London and spreading throughout the country.

More people were learning to read. That sparked a greater interest in books. Book stalls were springing up everywhere, even in railway stations. This interest encouraged better writers and artists to enter the field of publishing.

Edmund Evans, an engraver, had been quick to take advantage of this growing interest. He commissioned authors and illustrators to work for him. He printed books in red and blue ink on white paper. The white covers soiled easily, and the books did not sell well. Evans changed to a yellow paper with a shiny surface. This process was successful. The books were nicknamed "yellow backs" or "mustard plasters" by the public.

In the early days of publishing, it was the custom for the engraver to seek out a writer and an illustrator to discuss an idea that the engraver might have for a book. The engraver would then hire the writer and the illustrator to complete the book.

Evans visited Randolph to discuss a project. Walter Crane had illustrated a series of "toy" books for Evans. These picture books, which were meant to entertain children rather than to educate them, had become very successful. Evans wanted to publish more toy books, but Crane was not interested in illustrating more of them because he was busy designing wallpaper for the homes of wealthy people. Evans wished to print a series of picture books of nursery rhymes and folk poems. He had been greatly impressed with Randolph's illustrations in *Old Christmas*.

"I'm interested in illustrating the books for you," Randolph told him. "But rather than receiving a commission or flat sum, I would prefer to receive a set amount of money for each book sold."

"That is unheard of," Evans exclaimed. "Just how much did you have in mind?"

"A penny a copy," stated Randolph. "If the books do not sell, I receive nothing."

After a long and heated discussion, they agreed that Evans would pay all the costs for producing the books and that Randolph would receive a penny for each book sold. Two books would be published in the fall of each year, in time for the Christmas trade, for as long as they proved profitable.

The series began in 1878 with *The House that Jack Built* and *The Diverting History of John Gilpin*. These books were a great success. The first printing of 10,000 copies sold out before a second printing could be ordered.

In 1879, *An Elegy on the Death of a Mad Dog* and *The Babes in the Wood* were added to the series.

In 1880, *Sing a Song for Sixpence* and *The Three Jovial Huntsmen* were published.

The year 1881 saw the addition of *The Farmer's Boy* and *The Queen of Hearts*.

The Milkmaid and a single volume containing *Hey Diddle Diddle* and *Baby Bunting* were published in 1882.

A Frog He Would A-Wooing Go and *The Fox Jumps Over the Parson's Gate* were added in 1883.

In 1884, *Come Lasses and Lads* and a single volume containing *Ride a Cock Horse to Bambury Cross* and *A Farmer Went Trotting Upon His Grey Mare* were added to the list.

In 1885, the series ended with *An Elegy on the Glory of Her Sex, Mrs. Mary Blaize* written by Oliver Goldsmith and *The Great Panjandrum Himself*.

As each new title was added, the popularity of the previous titles increased until there were more than 100,000 copies printed. Randolph continued to receive a penny for each copy sold. It is believed that this agreement marked the first time that an illustrator was paid a royalty.

In 1879, the first four books were combined and published as *R. Caldecott's Picture Book: Volume 1*. In 1881, the second four books were combined and published as *R. Caldecott's Picture Book: Volume 2*.

In 1881, *R. Caldecott's Picture Book: Volume 1* and *R. Caldecott's Picture Book: Volume 2* were combined and published as *R. Caldecott's Collection of Pictures and Songs*.

In 1883, the third four books were combined and published as *The Hey Diddle Diddle Picture Book*.

In 1885, the last four books were combined and published as *The Panjandrum Picture Book*. Also, in 1885, *The Hey Diddle Diddle Picture Book* and *The Panjandrum Picture Book* were combined and published as *R. Caldecott's Second Collection of Pictures and Songs*.

A limited edition of 1,000 copies on larger paper, each copy numbered and autographed by Edmund Evans and the publisher, George Rutledge, was published in 1887 under the title *The Complete Collection of Randolph Caldecott's Pictures and Songs*. This edition sold out immediately. A few copies are still in existence today and are greatly prized by collectors.

The children loved the *Picture Books,* as Randolph and Evans called these volumes to separate them from the "toy" books. Randolph's skill as an artist carried the illustrations far beyond mere decoration. He interpreted the words. The illustrations were so complete that they practically told the story themselves.

The illustrations were also fun. The characters danced, sang, rode, or jumped their way across the pages. The children studied the pictures again and again to absorb all the marvelous details. Randolph's health was delicate and his manner quiet and serious. His illustrations were robust, bouncing with health. His characters, be they human or animals, simply surged with life.

Evans said of Randolph, "He is, by far, the most rewarding artist I have ever worked with."

While he was illustrating the *Picture Books,* Randolph met Marian H. Brind. They got married on March 18, 1880, in the Church of St. Martins-of-Tours, in Chelsford, Kent. The Brinds lived close to the church, and Marian walked to her wedding. Randolph's brother Alfred, who had become a priest as planned, assisted in the ceremony. Randolph and Marian settled down in the country at Wynbournes, Kemsing, a village near Sevenoaks.

These were the happiest days of Randolph's life. He was back in the country. He could delight, once again, in sketching animals and country scenes. His health was better than it had been in years.

For some reason, in 1882, Randolph and Marian decided to return to London. They left Wynbournes and took a long lease on a house at 24 Holland Street, in the Kensington section of London.

THEIR PARENTS BEING DEAD & GONE, THE CHILDREN HOME HE TAKES

From *Babes in the Woods*

Chapter 7

Randolph flowered in the prime of his career. He was a tall, handsome man. His curly brown hair still hung low about his forehead. His manner was still quiet and serious. The gaiety and humor buried deep within him, surfaced only in his drawings.

The house at 24 Holland Street was turned into a permanent studio within a year. Randolph and Marian missed the country so much that they settled into another country home in Farham, Surrey, within commuting distance of London.

The *Picture Books* continued to be published, two each year. Randolph delighted in this work. When Evans suggested the title *Babes in the Woods,* Randolph drew himself for the illustration of the line, "A gentleman of good account, soresick and like to die." The reviews in *The Nation* showed a lack of appreciation for that fact. The reviewer felt that Randolph had shown poor taste in treating a sad situation with humor. However, that illustration showed Randolph's awareness of his own poor health.

Traveling between Farham and London in a horse and buggy gave Randolph the opportunity to sketch much of the Surrey countryside into many of the *Picture Books.* Randolph kept to a rigid schedule while in Surrey. When he was not traveling to London, he rose at eight o'clock each morning and worked from ten until noon. Afternoons were spent walking, riding, or managing the small farm.

Through Thomas Armstrong, Randolph met Walter Crane, the illustrator of the "toy" books. Both Randolph and Crane came from old Chester families, although Crane had never lived there. The two men became close friends, visiting back and forth and discussing art techniques together.

Randolph also was acquainted with other illustrators whose work is still remembered today.

Kate Greenaway began her work about the same time as Randolph. Today, the two are often referred to as the "twin illustrators" because Greenaway was born in the same month and year as Randolph. They became friends and exchanged letters and visited each other. Greenaway was envious of Randolph's ability to take a short verse and develop illustrations that carried meaning beyond the words. She dearly loved his illustrations for "and the dish ran away with the spoon."

Beatrix Potter, the author and illustrator of *The Tale of Peter Rabbit* and other books, was a child at the time Randolph was illustrating the *Picture Books*. Her family encouraged her artwork. Her father purchased several of Randolph's original drawings for her to study. Two of the original drawings from *Sing a Song for Sixpence* today hang on the wall in her bedroom at *Hill Top*, two miles south of the village of Hawkshead, in the Lake District of England.

Randolph's success brought him more work than he could handle. Although his sketches gave the appearance of being completed quickly, he spent a great deal of time on each one. Whether the drawing was a full-page spread or a small action sketch, each line had to be perfect.

Marian became increasingly more concerned about Randolph's health. She wanted him to slow down, to spend more time relaxing and resting, but he had already committed himself to work that would take a full year to complete. And, although he agreed not to accept any new commissions, completing the work already promised began to affect his health. As he became more and more tired, he became less pleased with the results of his efforts. The drawings on paper would not match the images in his mind.

"Randolph, you must put away your work and rest," Marian insisted.

"I must finish what I have started," Randolph replied.

"Perhaps we should take Frederick's suggestion," Marian said. "You could rest and draw at the same time."

Frederick and Jane Locker-Lampson were close friends of the Caldecotts. Frederick had suggested a trip to the United States. The trip would be a combination of traveling and sketching, similar to the Harz Mountains trips.

"Perhaps you're right," Randolph decided, knowing that he could not continue his vigorous schedule. In addition to having a weak heart, he had tuberculosis and suffered from gastritis.

In 1885, the Caldecotts sold their lease at 24 Holland Street and prepared to sail for New York. Randolph was in fine spirits. The idea of a sketching trip throughout the United States appealed to him. It would open new vistas and provide vast new scenery. It might even improve his health.

From *The Diverting History of John Gilpin*

Chapter 8

Randolph stood at the rail of the Cunard steamship the *Aurania*. He breathed deeply of the fresh salt air and welcomed the cold fall wind blowing up close to a gale. For several days after leaving England, both he and Marian had been confined to their cabin with seasickness.

Now, Marian struggled to the rail beside him. Grasping dearly to the railing, she exclaimed, "I didn't think steamers this large would roll so. This is much worse than crossing the channel."

"The ocean is so large, the steamer but the size of the head of a pin," Randolph laughed. "I do hope they find an overland route by the time we make the trip back. Let's find shelter before you blow overboard."

Comfortably wrapped in blankets, in the lee of a smokestack, Randolph and Marian relaxed in deck chairs. The fresh air, combined with the swell of the rollers, lulled Randolph to sleep. Suddenly, he was moving along the deck toward the rail. Struggling, he threw off the blanket and with uneven steps fought his way across the deck and into the salon.

"That's enough of that," he declared to Marian, who had already sought the shelter of the salon.

The trip was long and tiring. Randolph sketched the passengers, the cabins during full gale, and the crew. He spent hours resting, but he did not feel rested. Twelve long days after leaving England, land was sighted, and the passengers crowded the deck.

Randolph's interest was caught by a young boy dressed like a miniature adult in a suit and topcoat.

"Look at that lad," Randolph pointed out the boy to Marian.

"He looks too young to even be out of the nursery," Marian said, shaking her head.

"That may be," answered Randolph. "However, he has been doing the Grand Tour of Europe all by himself."

"What can American parents be thinking of!" Marian was shocked.

"He interests me," Randolph said. "I have made several sketches of him."

A representative of the *New York Graphic* met Randolph and Marian and took them to their hotel. He urged them to stay for a few days, but Randolph wished to travel at once to a warmer climate.

"We can visit in New York on our return," he told the representative. "It should be warmer then."

The Caldecotts boarded the train for the south the next morning. Their first stop was in Philadelphia. They were not impressed with the lavish display of shop signs and other commercial advertisements. The horse railways running along the main streets, giving a sense of extreme hustle and bustle, made them nervous, and the numerous telephone poles and wires reminded them of spider webs. However, they did like the clean streets and the red houses with white doors, gray shutters, and well-scrubbed steps. They remained in Philadelphia just long enough for Randolph to record a portfolio of sketches.

Traveling south, Randolph was not impressed with the large number of signs, keeping pace with the rail route and sporting advertisements. These signs were set up in fields some distance away from the train but were large enough to be seen and read easily. His sense of humor caused him to sketch a hunting scene using the billboards as jumps for the horses.

The next stop was Washington, D.C. The city was not crowded because Congress was not in session. Randolph walked around and found a few politicians in town gearing up for the coming elections. He enjoyed sketching them and the town. He wrote to a friend, "Washington is a fine town with imposing public buildings, and wide, clean streets."

The last stop before Florida was Charleston, South Carolina. Randolph was ill. The trip had completely exhausted him. Marian wanted to eliminate this stop, but Randolph wanted to do a few sketches of the city. These sketches would be his last.

Early in December, they reached St. Augustine, Florida, and settled at the Magnolia Hotel. Randolph was seriously ill. Marian wrote to Jane Locker-Lampson that the weakness of Randolph's heart had complicated what she referred to as a severe attack of gastritis.

Near the end of January, Randolph seemed to be recovering. He was eating better and gaining strength. A relapse occurred, however, and Randolph died on February 13, 1886.

Thomas Armstrong, receiving the news by cable on February 14, had the sad duty of informing Randolph's family and friends of his death.

Marian handled all of the details of arranging Randolph's funeral. There was no time for assistance from England. Randolph was buried in the Evergreen Cemetery in St. Augustine, Florida.

Today, the schoolchildren in St. Augustine put flowers on his grave for all of the children, past and present, who have delighted in the merry illustrations by Randolph Caldecott.

A memorial to Randolph was installed in the crypt of St. Paul's Cathedral in London. The tablet pictures a serene Breton child holding Randolph's picture.

From *The Milkmaid*

Chapter 9

Although Randolph Caldecott's life span was but a month short of forty years, his drawings have survived for more than one hundred years. He was responsible for changing the direction in illustrating books for children.

The dictionary defines the word "illustrate," "as to explain, to make clear or make an example of." Early illustrators did just that. They took the story or rhyme and drew a picture showing exactly what the words described. They could be called decorators.

Randolph interpreted the words and drew pictures that communicated meaning that was beyond mere decoration. Each of Randolph's sketches surged with life. It is not enough to look once at his sketches and then to turn the page. One must look again and again to absorb all the details. One must notice the twinkle in the eye, the flash of a tail, and the expression of the animals watching the humans. And, one must watch the demure children, on the brink of breaking into a run as soon as the page is turned, and the human qualities of the dish running away with the spoon.

The *Picture Books* were Randolph's greatest contribution. Had it not been for them, he would have taken his place in history as a fine, but not a great artist.

In 1921, Frederick Melcher, President of the American Booksellers Association, proposed that the American Library Association sponsor an award to honor excellence in children's literature. The proposal was accepted and the Newbery Award, named after John Newbery, an eighteenth century book publisher, was established. René Paul Chambellan was commissioned to design a medal struck in bronze.

The Newbery Award had been in existence for fifteen years when Melcher proposed another award, one for excellence in picture books. This award would be given to the illustrator. The proposal was accepted by the American Library Association, and the Caldecott Award, named for Randolph Caldecott, was established. René Paul Chambellan was again commissioned to design a medal. He incorporated Randolph's own work into the design. He chose the illustration for John Gilpin's ride for the front of the medal and the pie with four and twenty blackbirds being set before the king for the back of the medal.

The first Caldecott Medal was presented to Dorothy Lathrop on June 14, 1938, for her picture book *Animals of the Bible.*

Today, the winners of the Newbery and Caldecott Awards are announced at the mid-winter meeting of the American Library Association.

When winners of the Caldecott Award are announced, Randolph Caldecott lives again as works by present-day illustrators are compared to sketches by the quiet, serious man whose love for children, animals, and the English countryside spilled off the pages into our lives and hearts.